Lila and Andy learn about Digital Networks

How the Internet Connects Us

Kenneth Adams

Book Cover by Kenneth Adams
Illustrations by Kenneth Adams
First Edition 2025

ISBN: 978-1-998552-14-6

A curious mind is never bored.

This book belongs to:

Hi guys, it's us, Lila and Andy again! Sharing information is our favorite thing, and we absolutely love spending time with you. We learn best when we learn together, and that makes it even more fun!

Today, we want to tell you about something amazing that surrounds us - digital networks!

When you write a note to your friend in class and pass it through different classmates until it reaches your friend, you're creating a path for information to travel. That path is actually a kind of network! Digital networks work the same. They form paths for information to flow through, except they're much faster and can reach anywhere in the world!

Just like a note passed through several hands, information on digital networks travels through different computers and devices. The big difference is that digital messages can travel near the speed of light! That's why a message to someone on the other side of the world arrives almost instantly.

Digital networks can send voice messages, pictures, videos, games, and many other types of information to millions of people at once!

The Basic Idea of Networks

Computers use a special language to talk with each other. It's called binary code, and it consists of just two numbers, 0 and 1. When computers send messages, they change everything, including words, pictures, videos, and even your favorite game, into long strings of zeros and ones.

Let's explain how cool this is. When you type the letter 'A' on your keyboard, your computer turns it into '01000001' in binary. It then sends this binary code through the network to another computer, which can turn it back into the letter 'A'. This happens with every single letter you type, and it happens so fast that you don't even notice it.

The really amazing part is that computers can send millions of these binary messages every second. That's why you can watch videos without waiting, play online games without delay, and send messages that arrive almost instantly. It's all done with tiny electrical pulses in cables or radio waves you can't see!

The Internet is the biggest and most amazing digital network ever created. It can connect every computer, phone, and tablet in the world to form a giant web that stretches across the entire planet. That's billions of devices!

While we think of the Internet as one thing, it's actually made up of many smaller networks that are connected together. Think of it like cities connected by highways, but instead of roads, we have cables, which carry information instead of cars.

These cables are large enough to carry massive amounts of data. Most cables are buried underground, and some run across the ocean floor to connect different continents.

Did you know the longest underwater cable is about 24,000 miles or 39,000 kilometers long? That's almost long enough to wrap around the Earth!

When you use the Internet, you can connect to computers in different countries without even knowing it.

For example, when you watch a video of an adorable puppy, the video might be stored on a computer in Japan, the comments on a computer in California, and the advertisements on a computer in Europe.

The Internet connects all these pieces so quickly that it seems like they come from the same place.

Different Types of Networks

We use the Internet so much that almost everyone has a <u>home network</u> these days. By using a wireless, or Wi-Fi, router, all our devices can connect to the Internet at the same time. The router makes sure that all digital information is sent to the right devices in your house, and it manages multiple connections at once.

Home networks are quite advanced. Each new device that connects to the router gets a special address called an Internet Protocol (IP) address. An IP address is unique, meaning no two devices have the same address. This way, the router ensures messages can find their way to the right place. The routers can handle many devices simultaneously, such as phones, computers, gaming consoles, and even smart appliances like refrigerators.

Your home network can also create a Local Area Network (LAN). This means devices in your house can talk directly to each other without going through the Internet. That's why you can wirelessly print documents or stream videos from your phone to your computer.

Did you know the average home now has about 10 connected devices? That's a lot of digital conversations happening all at once!

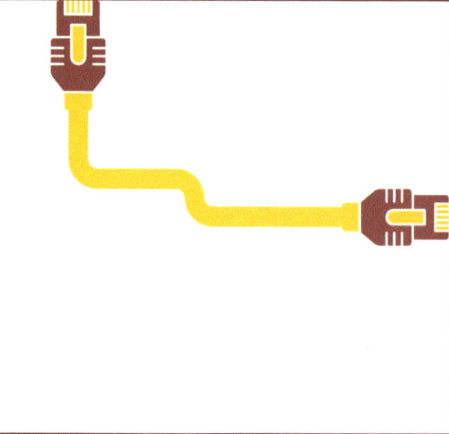

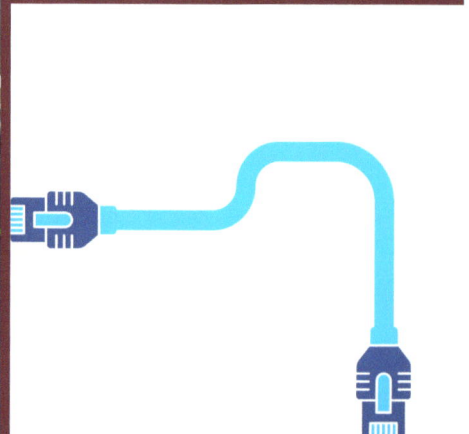

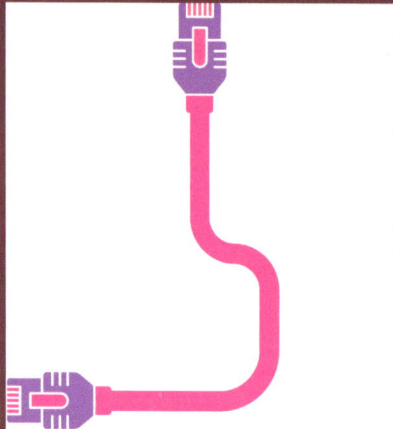

<u>School networks</u> work the same way as home networks but are much more significant. They can handle hundreds of connected devices, such as tablets and computers. This allows students to save their work on special computers called servers, have access to the same printers from different classrooms, and share learning materials across the whole school without having to move from classroom to classroom.

School networks can also have 'network segments.' This allows different classes, grades, or departments to have their own little part of the network that no one else can access. Teachers can share files only with their class, and the administration office can keep their files private.

Mobile networks are special networks that let our phones work anywhere we go. Unlike Wi-Fi, which only works when you're near a router, mobile networks use towers that send signals across entire cities. Each tower creates an invisible zone or coverage area around it, and all devices inside that coverage area connect to that specific tower. These zones are called 'cells,' which is why we call them cell phones! All the cells together form a network called a mobile network.

When you use your phone while moving around, it constantly talks to these towers. As you move from one cell to another, your connection jumps between towers to ensure you stay connected. This happens so smoothly that you won't even realize it.

These networks are not just useful for our phones. They're also important for things like self-driving cars and city services that rely on the Internet to work.

Did you know the latest mobile networks are called 5G? 5G is super fast and can relay information at up to 20 gigabits per second. That's fast enough to download an entire movie in just a few seconds!

Network Components

DEVICES

Gadgets that connect to networks are called 'network devices'. The most common ones are the devices you use every day, such as computers, phones, and tablets. Many smart devices, like smartwatches, thermostats, doorbells, gaming consoles, and even smart appliances like refrigerators and washing machines, can also connect to networks. This is part of something called the 'Internet of Things' (IoT). These devices can connect to the Internet and work on their own, making life easier! For example, a smart fridge can tell you when you're out of milk!

Each network device has something called a Network Interface Card (NIC) that helps it send and receive information over the network. Some devices need cables to connect, while others use wireless signals. Nowadays, most devices have both types built in, so they can use either method.

A useful feature of these devices is that they all understand the same digital language, called TCP/IP (Transmission Control Protocol/Internet Protocol). This allows all devices to talk to each other, no matter who made them or what they're used for. Thanks to TCP/IP, your Android phone can easily talk to your friend's Apple phone, or your gaming console can connect to a computer server on the other side of the world.

CONNECTIONS

The connections between network devices are like roads on which data travels. Some connections use physical cables. There are different types of cables, but the most common is an ethernet cable. These cables contain tiny copper wires or glass fibers that carry information using electrical signals or pulses of light.

Wireless connections use invisible radio waves to send information through the air. Wi-Fi is the most common type of wireless connection. It transmits data using specific frequencies that can pass through walls. This is why you can use Wi-Fi even when your router is in another room. However, the further the radio signal has to travel, the weaker it becomes and the slower the connection will be.

The fastest network connections worldwide use fiber optic cables. These cables are made of super-thin glass fibers that carry information as pulses of light. These amazing cables can transmit huge amounts of data across vast distances. The light signals bounce along the inside of the cable, traveling thousands of miles without losing strength.

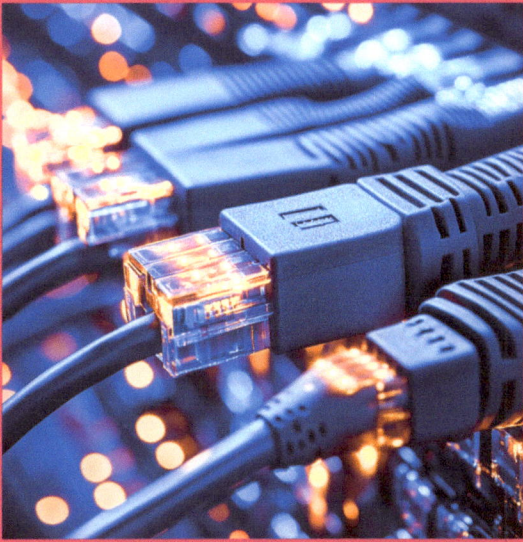

The twisted-pair design of ethernet cables was invented by Alexander Graham Bell in 1881 to reduce interference on telephone lines.

Wi-Fi travels slower through water! Your internet connection might weaken if you're using Wi-Fi in areas with high humidity.

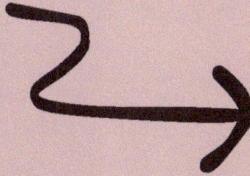

Optical fiber cables are so thin that a single strand is about the width of a human hair!

ROUTERS

Routers are the traffic wardens of the Internet because they help guide information to where it needs to go. When you send a message or request a website, the router figures out the best and fastest way your information should go.

Modern routers can handle thousands of connections at once and automatically choose the fastest path for each piece of information. If one path is too busy or not working, the router can instantly find another way to send the data. This is why the Internet keeps working even when some parts of it are broken.

Routers also help keep networks secure. They use Network Address Translation (NAT) to hide your device's real address from the Internet. It's like having a secret entrance to your house that only trusted visitors can use. Most routers also include firewalls that can block harmful traffic and protect your devices from cyber attacks.

SERVERS

Servers are like libraries because they store and share all kinds of digital information. When you visit a website, watch a video, or play an online game, you're actually connecting to a server. Servers are special computers designed to work 24 hours a day, 7 days a week, handling requests from millions of users.

Servers are located in special buildings called data centers. These centers are massive, some as big as several football fields. They need powerful cooling systems to prevent the servers from getting too hot and backup power supplies to keep everything running even if there's a power outage. Some big tech companies have data centers all around the world to ensure that their clients have access to their services quickly and without interruption.

Most big websites don't use just one server. They may have thousands of servers working as a team. When you stream a video, it will most likely come from the server closest to you, which makes it load faster. This network of servers is called a Content Delivery Network (CDN), and it's one of the reasons so many people can be on the Internet at the same time.

How Information Travels

MESSAGE PACKETS

When a digital message like a text or email is sent through the Internet, the information gets broken into tiny pieces of data called 'packets'. Each packet contains three important parts: a <u>header</u>, the actual <u>data</u>, and a <u>trailer</u>.

The <u>header</u> is like an address label that tells the network where the packet should go. The <u>data</u> contains a small part of the message you sent, and the <u>trailer</u> helps check if the packet arrived safely. The clever part is that each packet can take its own path through the network. If one path is too busy or broken, packets find different or alternative routes to the same destination.

The Internet Protocol (IP) address ensures that each packet knows where it needs to go. Another system, Transmission Control Protocol (TCP), ensures that all packets reach their destination and are put back together in the correct order. If any of the packets get lost along the way, TCP asks for them to be sent again.

When you type a website address into your web browser, the information might be split into hundreds of packets, all traveling and put together again in a fraction of a second. It happens so fast that you don't even notice it.

Sometimes, even though digital networks are fast, you might notice a delay when playing a game or watching a video. This delay is called 'latency,' and it happens when packets take longer to reach their destination. If the delay is too long, it can cause 'lag,' which makes games freeze or videos buffer.

FINDING THEIR WAY

The way packets navigate the Internet is quite impressive! Each packet has a unique IP address showing it where to go. As packets travel through the network, they encounter many routers that help them find the best route to their final destination.

Every router on the Internet communicates with its neighboring routers and tracks the best paths to different destinations. When a packet arrives, the router examines its heading to determine where it needs to go and then finds the fastest route to that location. It's like Dad using the navigation system in your car to find the best and quickest way somewhere.

Packets from the same message might take completely different paths, but they all end up at the same place. The Internet was designed this way on purpose. If one path becomes blocked or too slow, the packets search for other routes. This makes the Internet very reliable and hard to break.

Imagine you've built an airport out of building blocks. Your friend, who lives across the country, wants the same airport. Since you can't send it all at once, you break it down and mail it block-by-block in separate envelopes. Some take a direct route, while others pass through different post offices. When your friend receives all the envelopes, they carefully follow your instructions to rebuild the airport. In the end, it looks exactly like the one you sent.

That's how data packets travel over the Internet. They may take different paths but arrive at the same destination to be put together in the correct order again.

SPEED AND BANDWIDTH

The speed of Internet connections depends on bandwidth. Think of bandwidth as a pipe carrying water. The bigger the pipe, the more water can flow through it. More bandwidth means more data can flow through your connection at once.

We measure bandwidth in bits per second (bps). A connection with 100 megabits per second (Mbps) can transfer data at a rate of 12.5 megabytes per second (MBps). That's like downloading a whole song in less than a second.

Many factors influence the Internet speed you experience on your device, such as the type of connection (cable or Wi-Fi), the type of cable you are using (fiber optic or coaxial), how many people are using the network at the same time, and how far you are from your Internet provider's equipment.

Did you know the current record for the fastest fiber optic transmission is 319 terabits per second? That's fast enough to download 80,000 movies in just one second!

Internet bandwidth can be compared to a highway. Greater bandwidth allows more data to travel smoothly, just as a wider road allows more cars to travel simultaneously. Lower bandwidth, like a narrow road, limits data flow and can result in slower downloads and poorer performance.

Network Safety

PASSWORDS AND SECURITY

Keeping your network safe is very important. A password is like the keys to your house. Just like you wouldn't give your house key to strangers, you need to protect your passwords. You should select passwords that are hard to break. Strong passwords should be at least 12 characters long and include a mix of letters, numbers, and symbols.

Did you know that the most common password in the world is still '123456'? That's like leaving your front door wide open!

Modern networks use encryption to protect your information. Encryption works like writing a secret message in a special code that only trusted people can read. When you send a message online, your device scrambles it into a secret code, and only the receiver's device has the key to unlock and read it. The encryption used in modern Wi-Fi networks is so strong that it would take a supercomputer millions of years to crack it.

Many networks now also use two-factor authentication (2FA). This is like having a second lock on your door. Even if someone figures out your password, they still need a second code to get in, usually sent to your phone or email. This makes your account much safer.

PUBLIC AND PRIVATE NETWORKS

When you connect to the Internet away from home, you might use the Wi-Fi at a coffee shop or library. This is called a public network because it's open to the public. While these networks can be convenient, they're not as safe as your private network at home. It's like talking privately in your room versus in a crowded park where everyone can hear you.

Avoid online banking or entering passwords to access apps or websites when on a public network. When you need to use sensitive websites while on public Wi-Fi, use a Virtual Private Network (VPN). A VPN creates a secure, encrypted tunnel for your data, hiding your online activity from strangers.

Private networks, like home Wi-Fi, use special security features to protect your information. They have a firewall that acts like a security guard, checking everything that tries to enter or leave your network. The firewall also uses encryption to scramble your data so others can't read it. Most home networks use Wi-Fi Protected Access 3 (WPA3) encryption, currently the strongest security protocol available for Wi-Fi.

Think of public and private networks like the ocean and an aquarium. Devices on public networks are like fish in the open ocean. They're free to move around and do their thing, but they're also exposed to all sorts of dangers. Private networks, on the other hand, are like aquariums. They provide a safe and controlled environment where trusted devices can interact without worrying about dangers from outside.

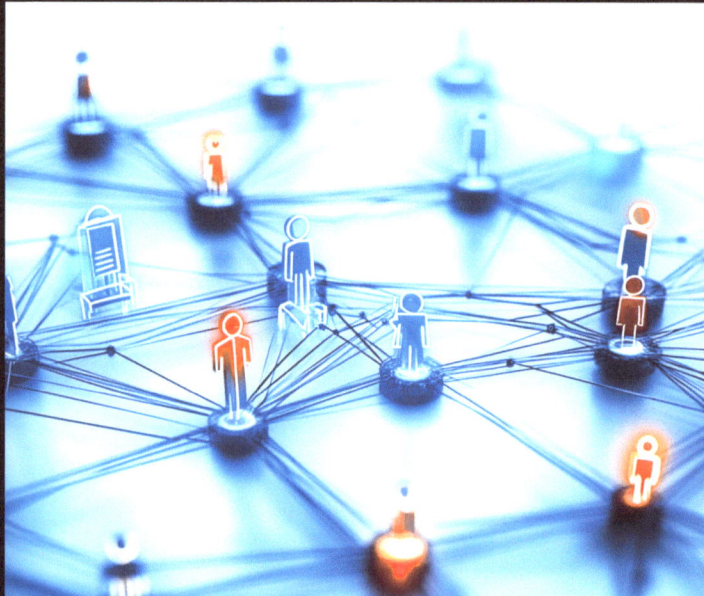
Don't use public computers for private stuff.

Did you know cyberbullying is a serious issue? Reporting harmful messages to your parents or blocking bullies can help keep you safer on the Internet.

Cybersecurity keep you safe from online attacks.

Hackers use their skills to access networks illegally to steal your information.

ONLINE SAFETY RULES

Staying safe online is not just about technical stuff like encryption and firewalls. You must also be very smart about what you share and do online. One important rule is never to share personal information like your address, phone number, or birth date on public websites or with people you don't know. If someone is being mean or makes you uncomfortable, always tell Mom and Dad.

Another important rule is to be careful about what you download. Programs and files downloaded from the Internet might contain viruses or malware, dangerous software that can steal your information or damage your computer. Always ask your parents before you download apps or software from the Internet.

One of the newest threats is 'phishing,' where scammers try to trick you into giving them your personal information. They might send an email that looks like it's from someone you know and trust. If something seems suspicious, it's better to be safe and not click on any links or download any attachments!

We've taken quite a journey through the world of digital networks! From the tiny packets zooming through cables to the massive servers storing our favorite websites, networks make our digital world possible.

It's amazing to think that you use many of the technologies we discussed today every time you send a message, watch a video, or play an online game.

The really exciting part is that networks keep getting better and faster. Who knows what awesome new things we'll be able to do soon?

Remember, just like in the real world, staying safe online is super important. Having strong passwords and being careful with what you share online will help keep you and your information safe.

Thanks for learning about networks with us. Keep exploring, stay curious, and, most importantly, stay safe online!

Digital Networks Glossary

A <u>glossary</u> is like a mini-dictionary of terms with definitions.

Here's a glossary of terms used for <u>Digital Networks</u>.

<u>Access Point</u> – A device that allows wireless devices to connect to a network.

<u>Authentication</u> – A security process to verify a user's identity before allowing access to a network.

<u>Bandwidth</u> – The maximum amount of data that can be transferred over a network in a given time.

<u>Binary Code</u> – A system of 0s and 1s used by computers to process and store information.

<u>Bit</u> – The smallest unit of digital data, represented as a 0 or 1.

<u>Bluetooth</u> – A short-range wireless technology used to connect devices like phones and headphones.

<u>Cache</u> – A temporary storage area for frequently used data to speed up access times.

<u>Cloud Computing</u> – The use of remote servers on the internet to store, manage, and process data.

<u>Content Delivery Network (CDN)</u> – A network of servers that speeds up access to websites by storing copies of content in multiple locations.

Cybersecurity – Measures taken to protect networks and devices from cyber threats.

Data Center – A facility that houses multiple servers for storing and processing data.

Data Packet – A small unit of data sent over a network, containing both the information and instructions on where it should go.

Decentralized Network – A network where no single computer or server controls all the data.

Digital Network – A system of interconnected computers and devices that share and transmit information electronically.

Domain Name – The name of a website (e.g., google.com), which is linked to an IP address.

Domain Name System (DNS) – A system that translates website names into numerical IP addresses.

Download Speed – The rate at which data is received from the internet.

Encryption – A method of scrambling data so that only authorized users can access it.

Ethernet Cable – A type of wired connection that links computers to a network.

Fiber Optic Cable – A high-speed cable that transmits data using pulses of light.

Firewall – A security system that prevents unauthorized access to or from a network.

Gateway – A device that connects two different types of networks.

Hacker – A person who gains unauthorized access to networks or computers.

Host – A device (such as a computer or server) that provides resources and services on a network.

Hotspot – A location that provides wireless internet access.

IP Address (Internet Protocol Address) – A unique set of numbers assigned to each device on a network.

ISP (Internet Service Provider) – A company that provides internet access to homes and businesses.

Latency – The delay between sending and receiving data over a network.

LAN (Local Area Network) – A network that connects devices in a limited area, such as a school or home.

Load Balancer – A device or software that distributes network traffic across multiple servers to improve performance.

MAC Address (Media Access Control Address) – A unique identifier assigned to network devices.

Malware – Malicious software designed to harm computers or networks.

Mesh Network – A network where devices are interconnected and pass data to each other without a central router.

Mobile Network – A wireless network that connects devices via cell towers.

Modem – A device that connects a home network to the internet.

Network Adapter – A hardware component that allows a device to connect to a network.

Network Interface Card (NIC) – A hardware component that enables a device to communicate with a network.

Phishing – A cyber attack where scammers trick people into revealing personal information.

Ping – A network test that measures the time it takes for data to travel from one computer to another.

Router – A device that directs internet traffic to the correct destination.

Scalability – A network's ability to grow and handle more devices or traffic.

Server – A computer that stores and manages network resources, such as websites and files.

Streaming – The continuous transmission of audio or video content over the internet.

Switch – A network device that connects multiple devices and directs data to the correct recipient.

TCP/IP (Transmission Control Protocol/Internet Protocol) – The main set of rules governing how data is transmitted across the internet.

Traffic – The amount of data moving through a network at a given time.

Upload Speed – The rate at which data is sent from a device to the internet.

Virtual Private Network (VPN) – A secure, encrypted connection that protects online activity from hackers.

Wi-Fi – A technology that allows wireless internet connections.

WPA3 (Wi-Fi Protected Access 3) – The latest encryption standard for securing wireless networks.

Digital Networks Quiz

Here's a quick quiz to test what your learned.

<u>Multiple Choice</u>

1. What is the basic language that computers use to communicate?
    a) English
    b) Morse Code
    c) Binary Code
    d) Digital Script

2. What does a router do in a network?
    a) Stores websites
    b) Directs internet traffic
    c) Translates languages`
    d) Blocks all connections

3. What is the purpose of an IP address?
    a) To identify a device on a network
    b) To store passwords
    c) To protect against hackers
    d) To boost internet speed

4. Which of these is an example of a wired connection?
    a) Bluetooth
    b) Wi-Fi
    c) Ethernet
    d) Satellite

5. The fastest type of internet connection uses:
    a) Fiber optic cables
    b) Copper wires
    c) Radio waves
    d) Telephone lines

6. What does LAN stand for?
    a) Local Area Network
    b) Large Access Node
    c) Long Automated Network
    d) Linked Antenna Network

7. What does DNS (Domain Name System) do?
    a) Speeds up the internet
    b) Translates website names into IP addresses
    c) Blocks harmful websites
    d) Connects devices to Wi-Fi

8. Which device allows multiple devices to connect wirelessly to a network?
    a) Router
    b) Modem
    c) Firewall
    d) Server

9. What is the main difference between Wi-Fi and mobile networks?
    a) Wi-Fi uses cables, mobile networks don't
    b) Wi-Fi is only available at home, mobile networks are everywhere
    c) Mobile networks use cell towers, Wi-Fi uses routers
    d) There is no difference

10. What is phishing?
    a) A method to catch internet signals
    b) An online scam that tricks users into giving personal information
    c) A type of high-speed internet
    d) A way to send messages faster

11. What do computers send data in?
    a) Folders
    b) Packets
    c) Capsules
    d) Clouds

12. The biggest digital network in the world is:
    a) The Local Area Network (LAN)
    b) The Internet
    c) The Wi-Fi Alliance
    d) The Cloud

13. What is a server?
    a) A type of Wi-Fi signal
    b) A computer that stores and shares information
    c) A security system
    d) A mobile network tower

14. Which of the following improves network security?
    a) Strong passwords
    b) Leaving devices unlocked
    c) Using simple passwords like "123456"
    d) Sharing passwords with friends

15. What is the function of a firewall?
    a) To keep devices warm
    b) To block unauthorized access
    c) To increase internet speed
    d) To send messages faster

16. How do fiber optic cables transmit data?
    a) Through electricity
    b) Through sound waves
    c) Using light pulses
    d) Using air pressure

17. Which of these is a wireless technology?
    a) Ethernet
    b) Fiber optics
    c) Wi-Fi
    d) Coaxial cable

18. Which mobile network technology is the fastest?
    a) 3G
    b) 4G
    c) 5G
    d) 2G

19. What does a VPN do?
    a) Blocks pop-up ads
    b) Speeds up internet connections
    c) Creates a secure, encrypted connection
    d) Disables Wi-Fi

20. What are the small sections of a network in a school called?
    a) Routers
    b) Firewalls
    c) Network segments
    d) Servers

Fill in the Blank

21. The Internet is made up of many _____ connected together.

22. A _____ is a unique number that identifies a device on a network.

23. The _____ protocol ensures that data packets arrive in the correct order.

24. A _____ protects a network by blocking unwanted traffic.

25. Wi-Fi stands for _____ Fidelity.

26. A _____ translates web addresses (like google.com) into IP addresses.

27. _____ networks use cell towers to provide internet on the go.

28. Computers communicate using only _____ and _____ (binary code).

29. Packets travel across the internet at almost the speed of _____.

30. A _____ is a computer that stores and provides information to other devices.

31. If someone asks for your personal information online, you might be a victim of _____.

32. Home networks are connected by a _____, which distributes internet to devices.

33. The fastest internet connections use _____ cables to send data as light signals.

34. The _____ protocol encrypts Wi-Fi connections for security.

35. The amount of data that can be sent at once is called _____.

36. A router helps to send data to the right devices.

37. Wi-Fi is always faster than fiber optic cables.

38. Mobile networks rely on cell towers to function.

39. Encryption makes data easier for hackers to read.

40. All internet traffic moves at the same speed.

41. Public Wi-Fi is always safer than home Wi-Fi.

42. Phishing is a safe way to download files.

43. A VPN helps protect your online privacy.

44. Data packets can take different routes to reach the same destination.

45. The internet connects billions of devices worldwide.

Answer Key

Multiple Choice	Fill in the Blank	True/False
1. c	21. networks	36. True.
2. b	22. IP address	37. False.
3. a	23. TCP	38. True.
4. c	24. firewall	39. False.
5. a	25. Wireless	40. False.
6. a	26. DNS	41. False.
7. b	27. Mobile	42. False.
8. a	28. 0s. 1s.	43. True.
9. c	29. light	44. True.
10. b	30. server	45. True.
11. b	31. phishing	
12. b	32. router	
13. b	33. fiber optic	
14. a	34. WPA3	
15. b	35. bandwidth.	
16. c		
17. c		
18. c		
19. c		
20. c		

Take a look at other subjects Lila and Andy are learning about...

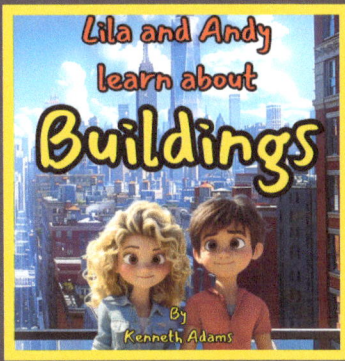

Lila and Andy learn about **Buildings**
By Kenneth Adams

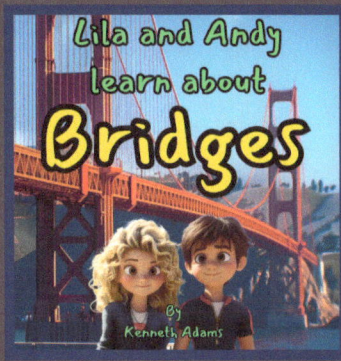

Lila and Andy learn about **Bridges**
By Kenneth Adams

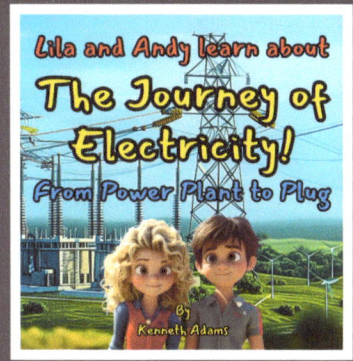

Lila and Andy learn about **The Journey of Electricity!**
From Power Plant to Plug

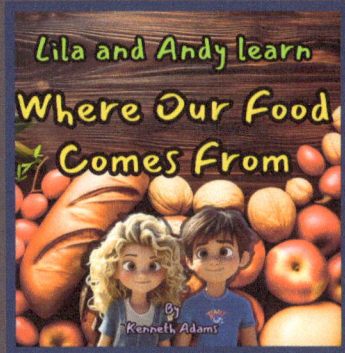

Lila and Andy learn **Where Our Food Comes From**
By Kenneth Adams

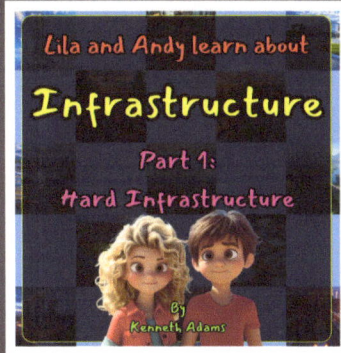

Lila and Andy learn about **Infrastructure**
Part 1:
Hard Infrastructure
By Kenneth Adams

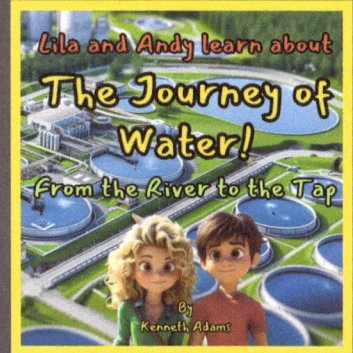

Lila and Andy learn about **The Journey of Water!**
From the River to the Tap

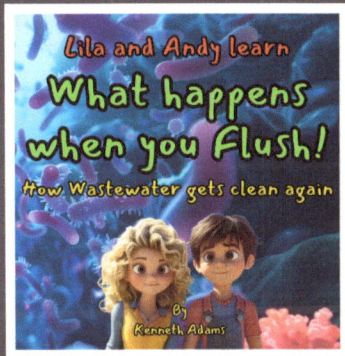

Lila and Andy learn **What happens when you Flush!**
How Wastewater gets clean again
By Kenneth Adams

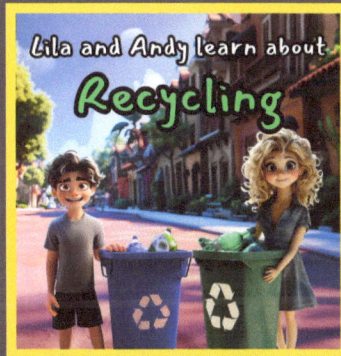

Lila and Andy learn about **Recycling**

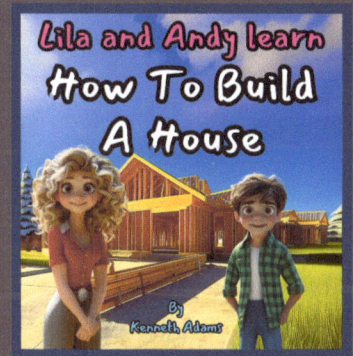

Lila and Andy learn **How To Build A House**
By Kenneth Adams

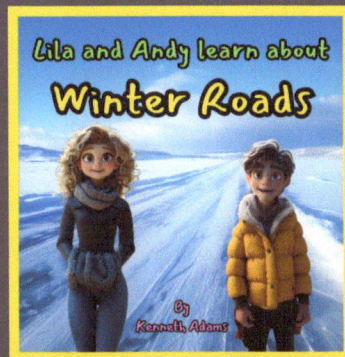

Lila and Andy learn about **Winter Roads**
By Kenneth Adams

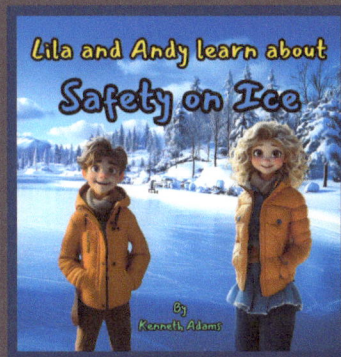

Lila and Andy learn about **Safety on Ice**
By Kenneth Adams

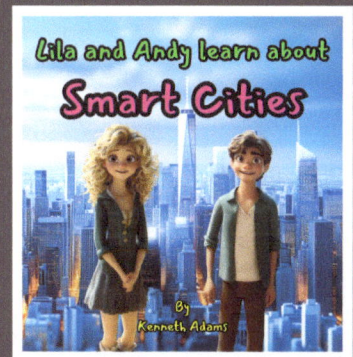

Lila and Andy learn about **Smart Cities**
By Kenneth Adams

www.ingramcontent.com/pod-product-compliance
Lightning Source LLC
LaVergne TN
LVHW072134070426
835513LV00003B/101